# Breathe with Thee

Poems from the Heart of God

## Terry Harris

Copyright © 2013 Terry Harris

All rights reserved. No part of this book may be used or reproduced by any means, graphic, electronic, or mechanical, including photocopying, recording, taping or by any information storage retrieval system without the written permission of the publisher except in the case of brief quotations embodied in critical articles and reviews.

WestBow Press books may be ordered through booksellers or by contacting:

WestBow Press
A Division of Thomas Nelson
1663 Liberty Drive
Bloomington, IN 47403
www.westbowpress.com
1-(866) 928-1240

Because of the dynamic nature of the Internet, any web addresses or links contained in this book may have changed since publication and may no longer be valid. The views expressed in this work are solely those of the author and do not necessarily reflect the views of the publisher, and the publisher hereby disclaims any responsibility for them.

Any people depicted in stock imagery provided by Thinkstock are models, and such images are being used for illustrative purposes only. Certain stock imagery © Thinkstock.

Scripture taken from the Holy Bible, New International Version®. Copyright © 1973, 1978, 1984, Biblica. Used by permission of Zondervan. All rights reserved.

ISBN: 978-1-4497-9598-6 (sc)
ISBN: 978-1-4497-9599-3 (e)

Library of Congress Control Number: 2013909250

Printed in the United States of America.

WestBow Press rev. date: 6/03/2013

This book is dedicated to my dear mother, Winifred Lynch, lovingly known as Winnie, who inspired me always, not only with a love for writing poetry, but with a love of our Savior Jesus Christ. She was an inspiration to all who knew her. She went to be with the Lord several years ago, and I still miss her terribly.

### Mother

There are many reasons why you're so special
But one thing is surely true:
In all His glory, in all His wisdom,
*God* made one very special *you*!

You were gently formed by the Master's hand,
And then He added your heart.
He filled it with so much love to give
That it truly sets you apart.

Your caring ways, your willing heart
Not only make you a mother.
Your love spills out to those around,
To every beautiful sister and brother.

We thank you for your abundant love,
Your special gifts that come from above,
Your smile, your concern, your love and caring,
The way you have of always sharing.
We thank you, Mother, for being *you*!

*Honor your father and your mother.*
—Exodus 20:12

## Acknowledgments

I would like to express my gratitude and appreciation to all those who walked with me from the original idea to the reality and completion of this book.

To my Lord and Savior, whose love for me overwhelms me completely. He has given me the gift of writing poetry, and I am humbled and amazed at His trust in me with His wonderful words. I am immensely grateful for His guidance at seeing this book to completion.

To my devoted and faithful husband, John, who has lovingly walked alongside me and believed in me for over forty years, and who loves the Lord and trusts Him completely.

To my wonderful children, Stephanie and Kimberly, and my precious grandchildren, Madison and Logan. They are the loves of my life, and I am so grateful for their support, love, and encouragement. They too have always believed in me.

To Ray and Judy Lynch, my brother and sister-in-love, who never doubted me or my desire to share my poetry with others. They are among my biggest encouragers.

To my numerous dear and special friends who have walked the walk with me and who have always encouraged me to publish my poetry. Their love has been an enormous blessing to me.

## Heartprints

God sends angels, our souls to touch,
Those whose lives we sometimes share.
With friends He blesses abundantly,
They are ones who truly care.

Many are those who cross our paths,
Many are those whose light shines bright.
But some leave a mark that we can't erase,
They leave a heartprint on the soul of our life.

*Now that you have purified yourselves by obeying the truth so that you have sincere love for your brothers,*
*love one another deeply, from the heart.*
—1 Peter 1:22

# Preface

For as long as I can remember, my mother wrote poetry. And for as long as I can remember, I wrote poetry too. In some ways it has always been easier for me to write poetry than prose. My mother had a box full of her poems, and after she passed away I was told that my brother had that box.

A few years later, I decided to take my mother's poems and publish them in honor of her. I was excited by my plan to give a copy to each family member for Christmas. However, when I called my brother to have him send me the box of poems, he said he did not have them. He thought all this time that I had them! This led to a frantic search. We both turned our houses upside down, but no poems. Regretfully, to this day we do not know what happened to them.

However, God used that loss to reignite my desire to write poetry. Feeling quite sad about the turn of events, I pleaded with God to show me what I could do about it. His response was an outpouring of poetry from Him through me. For months on end, He would fill my head with words of rhyme, and I would dutifully jot them down on paper. Some came to me at odd times, and I would have to run for a notepad and pen before I forgot the words.

Many of these poems are written from the overflowing of a joyful heart and the blessings that the Lord has bestowed upon me and upon my family. And some are the result of painful events and hard times as we strove to heal. Even others share God's creation in the special way in which He uses that to touch my soul.

Recently our family experienced the devastation of divorce. This began a more than two-year siege of pain and sorrow from which we are still healing. But again God used this experience to heighten my love for writing poetry, and He gave me many poems to put on paper as a result.

I am convinced that if I had found my mother's poems years ago, I never would have embarked on this journey of writing and publishing my poetry. Although I truly miss having my mother's poems, I am grateful to God for the time that He has allowed me to draw close to Him through my poetry.

These poems are not from my hand, but from God's. They are completely inspired by Him, and I am only blessed to be used by Him to hold the pen. I am humbled and grateful to be an instrument of God, used for His purpose. My only prayer is that all who read these poems will be inspired to draw closer to our Lord and Savior, Jesus Christ, and to put their trust completely in Him. He is waiting at your door for you to open it and to allow Him to enter your life and your heart. He wants you to trust Him completely and give your life to Him. That is my prayer for you. May God bless you always.

# Abundant Blessings

Many, many blessings
Abundantly I count.
They overflow, they gently pour
Like a water fount.

They come in great abundance
From the Father's hand.
They pour out all upon me
Like a million grains of sand.

Provision and protection
Are blessings from above.
His mercy and forgiveness,
His gift of grace and love.

The love of all my family
Blesses me in ways
That overfill my heart with peace,
With joy it fills my days.

My eyes to see creation,
Each sunset and new leaf;
My ears to hear my loved ones,
To run, with both my feet.

My hands that love to toil and work,
My lips to help me praise
My loving, heavenly Father
Throughout all of my days.

These are just a tiny few
Of all the blessings grand
With love and joy my Father pours
Like a million grains of sand.

## God's Creation

The sky so blue, the trees so green;
All around is so serene.
The breezes gently passing by,
The clouds so white up in the sky.

The birds' pure sound express God's joy.
A beautiful lilt of endless noise;
The birds' above melodious sound
From tops of trees to green grass ground.

Creation shouts of God's pure love,
It's seen around and up above.
His power and wonder all around,
Our Creator God does abound!

*And he swore by him who lives for ever and ever, who created the heavens and all that is in them, the earth and all that is in it, and the sea and all that is in it.*
—Revelation 10:6

## Needs and Wants

God has blessed us one by one
With all we'd ever *need*.
But in His grace and love for us,
He's added *wants*, indeed.

Sometimes we think our *wants* are *needs*—
How shameful to confess.
We're sorry, Lord, for times of greed
When we're so richly blessed.

We have everything we *need* today,
And most of what we *want*.
May our focus be not on our things,
But on our eternal life God bought.

*And my God will meet all your needs, according to His glorious riches in Christ Jesus.*
—Philippians 4:19

**Rain**

The rain comes down in bursts of sound
Pounding, pounding, not mere drips.
I struggle to see across the field,
But the view is blocked by a veil of gray.
Where does it go? Where does it flow?
It races with staunch determination.
Pounding, pounding, never stops,
This torrent rain; seems full of anger.
A wall of water from the sky
In streams of ribbon from high to low.
The puddles grow and grow.
Will the heavens continue to proclaim their power?
At some point it will stop
To reveal the glorious burst of sun,
To reveal God's proclamation of goodness:
The water and sun to nourish the beauty of His earth.

*He causes the sun to rise on the evil and the good, and sends rain on the righteous and the unrighteous.*
*—Matthew 5:45*

**Hope**

Our hope exists alone in Christ,
The ever-present sacrifice.
Our joy is in Him,
In Him alone.
For us and all
His love has shone.

What other hope?
Why, none at all!
Looking down from heaven,
The sin God saw.
But to our joy,
His hope He gave,
When Christ alone
Defied the grave!

For our sins and us
That day Christ died
To give us hope
By His sacrifice.

We now can be with God as one
And live forever with His Son.

*Find rest, O my soul, in God alone; my hope comes from Him.*
*—Psalm 62:5*

### God's Forgiveness

Your faithfulness, Lord, is awesome,
More than I can imagine,
Beyond comprehension.

How do I deserve it? I do not.
How can I earn it? I cannot.
How am I able? I am not.

Your forgiveness, Lord, humbles me,
More than I can imagine,
Beyond what I know.

How do I deserve it? I do not.
How can I earn it? I cannot.
How am I able to be forgiven?

By confessing to You, Lord.
You hear,
You listen,
You forgive.

By asking You to lead my life, Lord.
You hear,
You listen,
You make me Yours.

With humble gratitude, Lord.


*In Him we have redemption through His blood, the forgiveness of sins, in accordance with the riches of
God's grace that He lavished on us with all wisdom and understanding.*
—Ephesians 1:7

**Your Beauty Blesses Me**

I awake, I open eyes,
Your beauty I do see.
The sunshine bright
The sky so blue
Your beauty blesses me.

The day is fresh
So clean and new
The flowers smile
With morning dew
Your beauty blesses me.

Gone is the pain, also the rain
The clouds appear to part
The sun shines down without a sound
A new day now will start.

*Though I walk in the midst of trouble, You preserve my life.*
*—Psalm 138:7*

**God Loves the Color Blue**

In God's creation here on earth
He uses color full
To paint a glorious picture
On His canvas of the world.

He paints with colors vibrant
And some more muted still,
As with His huge artistic hand
He carries out His will.

So many colors everywhere,
But one I noticed true—
A hue most absent in my flowers
Is the color blue.

He paints a hundred flowers pink
And yellow, orange, red;
But not too many blue around
In the flowerbed.

But then I realized in awe
He does indeed love blue!
Look around at sky and water!
There's abundance of that hue.

So even though blue flowers are scarce,
God loves that color quaint,
But after painting water and sky,
He just ran out of blue paint!

*Shout with joy to God, all the earth!*
—Psalm 66:1

**Because of Thee**

Oh, broken am I,
So broken, I see.
How can that change?
What can change me?

Then God reaches down
From heaven above,
And I'm reconciled
By His forgiving love.

I am who I am,
Not because of me.
Oh, wondrous Lord,
It's because of Thee!

*Therefore, if anyone is in Christ, he is a new creation; the old has gone, the new has come!*
*All this is from God, who reconciled us to Himself through Christ.*
　　　　—2 Corinthians 5: 17–18

**The Day Christ Died**

That dark and dreary day Christ died
Upon the cross, a human sacrifice.
He suffered for us, our sins to bear,
And looks over us still with loving care.

Along the dusty road He bore
The cross, a symbol evermore.
Dying there, upon the hill,
Through pain and suffering, forgave them still.
With nails pierced through His hands and feet,
He kept that silent look of peace.

And as He died, to God He said,
"Father, forgive them, please forgive,
For they know not what they do."
May we feel that same way too.

May this remind us of that day
When rain from the storm washed away
The human blood of Jesus Christ
Upon the cross, a human sacrifice.

*Jesus said, "Father forgive them, for they do not know what they are doing."*
—Luke 23:34

## The Seed Planter

Often we're called to plant God's seeds,
Sometimes it seems boring to do.
We're not always around to see the results
Of the flower and fruit when it's new.

But if we failed to plant God's little seeds
At the time and the place He would choose,
Then the people in line to water and weed
Would not have a job to do.

And later in time at the spot God chose
Nothing but weeds would grow;
When actually God had planned for us
To be the start of a glorious show.

So remember we must, as we meet each day,
The importance of the Seed Planter's task.
And we will share together in God's beautiful plan
As we do everything that He asks.

*I planted the seed, Apollos watered it, but God made it grow.*
*—1 Corinthians 3:6*

**Have I Chosen God?**

Have I chosen God to lead me
Today and every day?
Or am I just trying to do it
In my very own small way?
Have I looked to Him in prayer
To direct my every move?
Or am I not asking Him
The way He said I should?

God is waiting every day
With patience, care, and love
To give me His strong hand
And lead me from above.
He promises to direct my life
Each day and every minute
As I accept His love and offer
With my life, and let Him in it.

If I will just allow the Lord
To lead me every day,
And seek Him in commitment
Through prayer, I can obey.
His love and will for me
Will be awesome and beyond
Whatever I think I could do
Without His saving Son!

*If I rise on the wings of the dawn, if I settle on the far side of the sea, even there Your hand will guide me,*
*Your right hand will hold me fast.*
*—Psalm 139:9-10*

**Worship**

Until we cease to worship things
And instead worship only the King of Kings,
We never can be satisfied
And find the peace that only He provides.

Things sometimes creep into our lives,
Taking the spot in our heart as it hides.
We're sure these things will bless us indeed
And fill an empty hole in need.

But until we cease to worship things
And instead worship only the King of Kings,
We never will be satisfied
And find the peace that He provides.

*Magi from the east came to Jerusalem and asked, "Where is the One who has been born king of the Jews? We saw His star in the east and have come to worship Him."*
—Matthew 2:2

## A New Place

God took me to a new place
Where I would never choose to go.
And in the process and the pain
He truly helped me grow.

I didn't want to be there,
The pain felt cold and great.
But onto God's big hand I held
And leaned upon His weight.

He carried me when things got hard,
He soothed my falling tears.
And always and forevermore
I could feel that He was near.

He was with me in the new place
I felt His strength and love.
He helped me grow and grow again
With His mercy from above.

*God will wipe away every tear from their eyes.*
—Revelation 7:17

## Awesome Beauty

Such awesome beauty all around,
It's hard to take it in.
Breathtaking and amazing;
Where does it all begin?

It begins with God alone, dear one,
The author of each part.
He created from His love for us
To share and touch our heart.

Each tiny flower, each sunset glow,
God gave us with His love.
In each and every part, we know,
He loves us from above.

*This is the day the LORD has made; let us rejoice and be glad in it.*
—Psalm 118:24

## As I Prayed Today

As I closed my eyes to pray today
I heard the chirping of the birds.
I am reminded of my ears
To hear God's glorious words.

My eyes I opened to reveal
God's creatures as they played.
I thank You, Lord, for eyes to see
Your creation every day.

How blessed I am with voice to share
While on my lap she sits.
My precious one watches all God's birds
With squeals of joy from her lips.

May I always use these gifts from God
Of ears and eyes and voice
To praise my great and glorious Lord
And always make this choice.

*Are not two sparrows sold for a penny? Yet not one of them will fall to the ground apart from the will of your Father.*
*—Matthew 10:29*

## Baby Boy

Baby boy so soft and sweet
From top of head to tiny feet.
God made of you each little part,
He loved you so right from the start.

He knew you from beginning of time,
With Him your little heart will shine.
God has an awesome plan for you,
Oh little boy dressed up in blue.

God knows each minute of your life,
He'll guide you always, day and night.
God made of you each little part,
He loved you so right from the start.

*Jesus called the children to Him and said, "Let the little children come to Me, and do not hinder them, for the kingdom of God belongs to such as these."*
*—Luke 18:16*

## Your Creation Blesses Me

Thank You, Lord, for sunshine bright.
Thank You for the pale moonlight.
Thank You for the cooling rain
Across the meadow and the plain.

Thank You, Lord, for beaches white,
For stars that grace the sky at night.
Thank You, Lord, for flowers aglow
That beautify the field just so.

Thank You, Lord, for mountains tall.
Thank You for the birds' sweet call.
Thank You, Lord, for all I see;
Your creation truly blesses me.

*For by Him all things were created: things in heaven and on earth.*
*—Colossians 1:16*

# Trust

Direction for my life today
Comes through God's opened doors.
He opens them with His big hand
To move me through, and more.

"This is the path I have for you,"
God seemed to say that day,
And every door that I went through
Brought joy in following God's way.

With each and every confirmation
God gave from His whole heart,
All I had to do was pray
And be obedient for my part.

But then one day, a door slammed shut.
How can that really be so?
I thought I followed God's commands
As through each door I'd go.

God has reached a time today
Where closing a door He must,
To teach His special gift to me,
And that gift is to trust.

All opened doors were not, alone,
His total will for me.
And it was hard and difficult
His will for me to see.

But in His precious love and care
God gave a special sign.
A rainbow over top my house
Gave me a special calm.

He showed His deep abiding love
And also a lesson true.
He asked me simply Him to trust
And trust in Him I do.

*Trust in the LORD with all your heart and lean not on your own understanding; In all your ways acknowledge Him, and He will make your paths straight.*
—Proverbs 3:5–6

**Each New Day**

Each morning is a new day,
A new day from the start.
The past is gone, it is no more,
It lives only in my heart.

Lord may I always in faith begin
Each beautiful new day
By praising You and thanking You
For Your loving, caring way.

I love You, Lord, I trust You
With each part of my day.
May I never fail to let You lead
My life in every way.

*This is the day the LORD has made; let us rejoice and be glad in it.*
—Psalm 118:24

**Like Jesus**

Can I be like You, dear Jesus,
In all I do and say?
Will I be like You, dear Jesus,
When meeting others today?

Help me, Lord, to be like Thee,
With kindness in my heart.
When others hurt or feel alone,
Help me Your love impart.

With love in word, with helping hand,
With unexpected pleasures;
If I let the Holy Spirit lead
I can give of myself beyond measure.

Yes, I could be like You, dear Jesus,
In all I do and say.
But I must first give my heart to You
To be effective in every way.

*For we are God's workmanship, created in Christ Jesus to do good works,
which God prepared in advance for us to do.*
—Ephesians 2:10

**You First, Lord**

Lord, help me always put You first.
You alone, Lord, first in my life;
First in my thoughts,
First in my prayers,
First in all I am.

Oh, Lord, forgive those times of selfishness;
Of selfish thoughts,
Of selfish prayers,
Of selfish all.

You alone, Lord, deserve my best:
My best thoughts,
My best prayers,
My all for You, Lord.

Oh, Lord, may I always put You first.

*But seek first His kingdom and His righteousness, and all these things will be given to you as well.*
—Matthew 6:33

**Forgive Me, Lord**

Forgive me, Lord.
I didn't let You in my life today.
But You are always there for me
Even when I fail to pray.
Forgive me, Lord.

Amazing though You are,
You never once forget me.
So how do I fail You, Lord,
When with You I want to be?
Forgive me, Lord.

*Bear with each other and forgive whatever grievances you may have against one another.*
*Forgive as the Lord forgave you.*
—Colossians 3:13

## God's Strength and Love

The night, Oh Lord, is darkest
Just before the dawn
When grief's intense engulfing
Around and o'er me swarms.

The pain is cold and crushing
It sears my very soul.
How can I break this feeling
That grabs me and takes hold?

Oh, Lord, I know You're out there
But You seem so far away.
Will You please hold me always
And take my pain away?

Yes, dear one, I'm holding you,
I love you more than life.
I bear your pain upon Me
In the darkest night.

And the night, dear one, is darkest
Just before the dawn,
But I have an awesome plan for you,
A good and special one.

Trust in Me, dear child of Mine,
Though so hard it is today.
My strength and love surround you,
As in My arms you stay.

I love you so, dear child of Mine,
Please rest in My strength and love,
And I will pour My peace on you
In abundance from heaven above.

## My Special Little Child of Mine

My special little child of Mine,
Created for My light to shine.
I hold you tight, I love you so,
I watch you as you come and go.
My purpose you will fill divine,
My special little child of Mine.

My special little child of Mine,
How could you know My plan in time?
Do not doubt for a single minute
That you are where I want you in it.
My plan was made with you in mind,
My special little child of Mine.

I looked from heaven to earth below
And sought to find a place just so
For My special little child of Mine.
A place with care where you can shine,
A place where love and grace abound,
Where praise to Me is familiar sound.

My special little child of Mine,
I watch with care, My ear inclined.
Where would this place of solace be,
A place of love for the world to see?
This place I found for you, dear one,
Is filled with Jesus, God's dear Son.

My love will rest on you, My child.
There's joy and peace and hope inside.
This place is what I built for you,
Built for you and your family too.
A place of respite for you to shine,
My special little child of Mine.

*Jesus said, "Let the little children come to me, and do not hinder them, for the kingdom of heaven belongs to such as these."*
*—Matthew 19: 14*

**My Savior's Love**

My Savior's love
So pure, complete;
I bow me now
At Jesus' feet.

A love so great,
So freely given,
Upon the cross
He gave me heaven.

My Savior's love
So pure, complete;
I bow me now
At Jesus' feet.

Though undeserved,
Though full of sin,
God's love so great
Allowed me in.

My Savior's love
So pure, complete;
I bow me now
At Jesus' feet.

*But when the kindness and love of God our Savior appeared, He saved us, not because of righteous things we had done, but because of His mercy. He saved us through the washing of rebirth and renewal by the Holy Spirit, whom He poured out on us generously through Jesus Christ our Savior, so that, having been justified by His grace, we might become heirs having the hope of eternal life.*
—Titus 3: 4–7

**God's Abundant Peace**

Peaceful water, oh so still,
Sharing all God's loving will,
Over rock and under tree,
God has abundant peace for me.

Peaceful water flowing strong
Over rocks it flows along.
As it passes by a tree,
It shares God's abundant peace for me.

By water's edge I feel God's love,
I feel His strength from up above.
What joy behold its beauty see,
God shares abundant peace with me.

*He leads me beside quiet waters, He restores my soul.*
—Psalm 23:2

**Love**

My Lord, how I love Thee!
Amazing strength I receive from You.
Awesome love blesses me every day.
Oh, Lord, I can feel Your loving arms around me;
Arms of strength,
Arms of protection,
Arms of love.
On You can I cast all my cares,
On You can I lean for all time.
Your strength and love overwhelm my very soul.
Forever, Lord, You are there for me.
Forever, without condition, is Your love for me.
How awesome is Your strength and love, oh my Lord!
How grateful am I for You!

*Love the Lord your God with all your heart and with all your soul and with all your mind.*
*—Matthew 22:37*

**Open My Eyes**

Lord, open my eyes that I may see
All the beauty You have for me.
The wonders, Lord, of brilliant snow,
The glorious red of sunset glow.

The flowers blue and pink and yellow,
The waters green, so calm and mellow.
Your glory seen in stars above,
Your Spirit in the soft white dove.

Lord, open my eyes that I may see
All the beauty You have for me.
Make me mindful, Lord, today,
Through your creation, of all You say.

*No eye has seen, no ear has heard, no mind has conceived what God has prepared for those who love Him.*
*—1 Corinthians 2:9*

**The Storm**

There are times in life when winds blow strong.
It's hard to see, it's hard to move on.
The Lord is near, though it's hard to feel,
And it seems our very soul it steals.

At times like this when all is worn
It's so hard to praise Him in the storm.

When all seems lost and our hearts do break,
When tears stream down for others' sake,
The Lord is near, though it's hard to feel,
And it seems our very soul it steals.

At times like this when all is worn
It's so hard to praise Him in the storm.

As we go through struggles that cause us pain,
Or if we watch others whom we love lose gain,
Praise God; we truly know He's there,
Watching over us with loving care.

And most of all, when we feel worn,
He knows it's hard to praise Him in the storm.

But praise God this day and His loving will
As He wraps us tight and holds us still.
Praise God we truly know He's there,
Watching over us with loving care.

And most of all, when we feel worn,
He holds us as we praise Him in the storm.

*Blessed is the man who perseveres under trial, because when he has stood the test, he will receive the crown of life that God has promised to those who love him.*
—James 1:12

**His Best**

Clouds of fluffy white and gray
Against a clear blue sky;
I look above, am overwhelmed—
I know the reason why.

Each fluff of white, each wisp of gray
Tells of the story true.
God alone creates it all
On His awesome canvas blue.

Such beauty I behold today
Above from east to west.
God has in all His glory shown
For us to see His best.

*One generation will commend Your works to another; they will tell of your mighty acts.*
*They will tell of the power of Your awesome works.*
*—Psalm 145: 4, 6*

**Breathe with Thee**

Forgive me, Lord,
I rush through life,
I look but do not see.
Help me, Lord, to take the time,
In peace, to breathe with Thee.

In rush and plans
I walk too fast,
I follow only me.
Help me, Lord, to take the time
To sit and breathe with Thee.

When life becomes
More pain than peace,
And sadness all have we,
Help me, Lord, to take the time
To share and breathe with Thee.

I look around
My focus lost
When naught I lean on Thee.
Please help me, Lord, to stop right now,
And love and breathe with Thee.


*And with that He breathed on them and said, "Receive the Holy Spirit."*
—John 20:22

# I Trust in You

I trust in You when things are low,
I trust when things go awry.
I look for strength when all is lost,
The times when I ask *Why?*

You walk beside me every day,
You hold my hand so tight.
You carry me when I've no strength,
You're with me day and night.

When times seem dark and oh, so bleak,
You're there as I sadly kneel.
Then as I walk along, step by step,
Your strength is what I feel.

You hold me tight, You love me,
You tell me not to fear,
And as You walk along with me,
You whisper in my ear.

You tell me to be hopeful,
For what You need of me
Is a broken heart completely,
Then Your work I'll clearly see.

One day when I awaken,
It's true that I will see
Your strength and love were all I needed,
When the days were bleak.

But now I've passed the darkness through,
The light now brightly shines,
And You have blessed me abundantly
With blessings that are mine.

I thank you, Lord, for loving me,
And walking far and long
Through the path You laid for me—
It helped to make me strong.

I pray that as I walk through life
With trials that will surely come
I'll always remember the way to walk
Is with Jesus, God's dear Son.

*The LORD is close to the brokenhearted and saves those who are crushed in spirit.*
—Psalm 34:18

**Everywhere**

God is present in the waters still,
God again in the whippoorwill.
Even God in the clouds of gray
God is everywhere day by day.

The leaves of gold on the oak so tall,
God is there in His all and all.
Birds of the sky and gulls in the air—
God, my God, is everywhere!

*For everything God created is good.*
*—1 Timothy 4:4*

**Birds**

Provision, protection by Your power and might;
The peace of creation, a seagull takes flight.
Your wonder and mercy and grace from above;
Your beauty, oh Lord, on the wings of a dove.

You bless us, dear Father, more than we deserve,
With Your gift of our ears, we enjoy the birds:
The chirp and the twitter of their melodious sounds
As they sit in the trees and walk on the ground.

How peaceful, how gently Your creation does bless
As we watch the geese move to their waterside nests.
With goslings protected and trailing behind,
They follow along in the straightest of lines.

*Look at the birds of the air; they do not sow or reap or store away in barns,
and yet your heavenly Father feeds them. Are you not much more valuable than they?*
—Matthew 6:26

**God's Beauty**

God's awesome beauty all around;
I hardly can perceive
All that God has given me.
But I do believe
In all His power and all His might—
My eyes so clearly blessed.
Upon His glorious creation
God's beauty brings me rest.

The peace of His creation
Blesses my very soul.
But only God and God alone
Can truly make me whole.

*He has made everything beautiful in its time.*
—Ecclesiastes 3:11

**Hats of White**

Hats of white on posts of brown,
Fluffs of white all around,
A feather bed, the countryside,
Popcorn balls far and wide.

*Slish*, *slosh*, melt, drop
From the trees in the breeze.
Once again, God's hand I see
In His beauty that surrounds me.

*Cleanse me with hyssop, and I will be clean; wash me, and I will be whiter than snow.*
—Psalm 51:7

**Peaceful River**

Peaceful river passing by
For everyone to partake;
Peaceful river washes clean
Every sin I make.

Peaceful flow of water clean
Draws me to Christ this day,
For He alone can make me new
In all I do and say.

The peace of river flowing,
The peace of Christ alone;
My heart doth take, my sins erased,
God's glory to be shown.

*For God so loved the world that He gave His one and only Son,*
*that whoever believes in Him shall not perish but have eternal life.*
—John 3:16

**God's Creatures**

The egret, so still in the water,
Then gently moves with purposeful strength.
The geese fly overhead,
The whirring of their wings in perfect harmony—
God's creatures graceful and strong.
I watch with peaceful appreciation
Of all that God has created.

*How many are Your works, O LORD! In wisdom You made them all; the earth is full of Your creatures.*
—Psalm 104:24

**God Alone**

Looking, looking
Seeking, seeking
Meaning
To this life of mine.
Where, oh, where,
Through toil and care,
Meaning to all will I find?
How to grasp
How to climb
Finding meaning one more time.

There it is!
All around
God's creation, every sound.
It's not *my* meaning
That will shine,
But God's alone
Throughout all time.

No, it's not in human toil—
It's God alone where I find joy!

*What does a man gain from all his labor at which he toils under the sun.*
—Ecclesiastes 1:3

## Christ's Love

Christ's love bursts forth from deep within
Our own repentant souls;
And it is true that God alone
Can truly make us whole.

At times we're self-sufficient—
A sin He cannot bear.
God reaches down, His hand stretched out,
Hoping that we'll care.

Will we truly care enough,
And say to Him "Oh, yes!
I love You, Lord, I give my life
To You—please make me blest.

"Make me blest for Christ, alone,
That I might serve only Him,
And not be self-sufficient, Lord,
Not ever, ever again!"

*I tell you, there is rejoicing in the presence of the angles of God over one sinner who repents.*
—Luke 15:10

*Be still and know that I am God.*
—Psalm 46: 10

CPSIA information can be obtained
at www.ICGtesting.com
Printed in the USA
LVIW02n0412041013
355358LV00002B